# Mother to Son

# Mother to Son

## Shared Wisdom from the Heart

by Melissa Harrison and
Harry H. Harrison, Jr.

Workman Publishing Company

New York

This book was twenty-six years in the making and is the product of the wisdom
of many outstanding moms. Charlotte Lee and Judy Birkes offered valuable insight.

Library of Congress Cataloging-in-Publication Data is available.
ISBN 978-0-7611-4210-2

Workman books are available at special discounts when purchased in bulk for
premiums and sales promotions as well as for fund-raising or educational use.
Special editions or book excerpts can be created to specification.
For details, contact the Special Sales Director at the address below.

Cover and book design by Paul Gamarello

Workman Publishing Company, Inc.
225 Varick Street
New York, NY 10014-4381
www.workman.com

16 15 14 13 12 11 10 9 8 7

# Preface

*"As a mother, my job is to take care of what is possible and trust God with the impossible."*
—Ruth Bell Graham

*"It's a boy."*

With these words, each mother starts a journey. This book is a guide to navigating the relationship— sometimes exhilarating, sometimes exasperating, but always extraordinary—between a mother and her son. The wisdom on these pages is designed to make you laugh, to make you sigh, and to give you strength. It's not easy to raise a loving, strong, and successful boy, but with each milestone—from the first bedtime story to the last day of school—you'll be reminded that you're doing the most important job in the world.

# The Five Keys

1. Pray for him every day.

2. Respect his father.

3. Do everything in your power to create a peaceful home.

4. Feed him love, morals, values, and integrity daily.

5. Be a strong woman.

# In the
# Beginning

Realize that your son will love
you more intensely than anyone
or anything else in the world.

At times, you will be blown away by the depth of your love for him.

Don't forget that as
a baby, he will always
be looking for your face.
It will be this way forever.

Spend as much time with him as you can. This is for your sake as well as his.

Read all the advice books and baby guides you want, but trust your instincts. They're good.

Watch out when you're changing his diaper. Baby boys shoot straight in the air.

Know that your job in life is to feed him, love him, and point him in the right direction.

Be ready for him to wake up hungry. Boys eat more than you can imagine, even as babies.

Keep lots of
soft towels handy.
He's a drooling machine.

The more you
talk to him, the sooner
he'll talk to you.

Don't talk to him
all the time in baby talk.

Realize that from day one,
he's wired to be self-reliant.
Don't change that.

If you wait until he
cries to pick him up,
you're teaching him to cry.

He will need a nap every day
for his first five years. So will you.

Accept the fact that boys and girls are different.

Steel yourself for when the doctor has to give him shots. His screams will wake the dead.

Baby-proof your home.
Anything he can reach,
he will put in his mouth.

You'll come to appreciate
baby shampoo as
one of the world's
greatest inventions.

You will want to just watch him—his eyes, his hands, his movements—for hours. It's normal.

Remember, he needs
to be around you,
to hear your voice,
to see you looking at him.

Relax.
Throwing food is normal.
Heck, throw it back.

Driving in a car will put him to sleep. Keep this in mind when it's 2 A.M. and he won't stop wailing.

Take him for walks.
Tell him what he's seeing.

You don't have to be a constant source of entertainment. Let him entertain himself. Everything is stimulating to babies.

Buy him a soft blanket.
He will keep it for years.

Keep in mind
that from the moment
he starts crawling,
he's tasted freedom.

Don't worry about falling off
your exercise program.
Once he starts walking,
you'll be chasing after him more
than enough to make up for it.

# Set up a college savings plan. Now.

You'll remember
his laughter at this
age forever.

Don't forget, he needs
one-on-one attention
from you.

Practice staying calm.
This will serve you well
in his teenage years.

For reasons unknown, he will want to sit in your closet and play with your shoes. For hours.

It's okay if he falls down.
What's important is that
he learns to pick himself up.

# The Toddler
# Years

Note that his idols
will always be boys
five years older than he is.

You'll be tempted to throw elaborate birthday parties for him, even when he's one or two or three. Don't.

Be consistent: with
your love, with rules,
with discipline.
With everything.

Try to make rules fun.

His tears will break your heart. So will his smiles.

Remember, boys tend to be competitive about everything. It will make no sense to you and sometimes scare you to death.

Don't panic over his eating
a bug or two. Boys just want
to know what things taste like.

Tell him to aim when he uses the bathroom. Until he does, he will hit everything *but* the toilet.

Remember, toddler
boys are terrors.
It goes with the age.

He will be itching
to go outside all the time.
Take him out.

If you make fun of him,
he'll learn to be shy.

Don't overreact when
he hurts himself,
and he won't either.

Try as you might,
you can't shield him
from life.

The sooner he learns to follow the rules, the easier his life will be. And yours.

He will become
unraveled when you leave
him with a babysitter.
Go quickly.

Introduce him to crayons and paint. But keep an eye on him or he'll redecorate your home.

Install safety catches on all
the cabinets he can reach.
This is as much for your sanity
as for his safety.

Right around the age of three, he will heroically start to think he is your protector. This never goes away.

If you want him to
listen to you when he's
a teenager, teach him
to listen to you now.

Nightmares can terrify him. Hold him, comfort him, and watch over him until he falls back asleep.

He'll continue to whine
for as long as it works.

From you, he'll learn the
importance of telling the truth.
Be a good model.

Remember these words:
*It's just a phase.*

Make him drink his milk. But don't make him clean his plate.

Don't skip naptime, or you will both pay dearly.

If you buy him something every time he goes to the store with you, you'll soon be buying him something every time he goes to the store with you.

Establish a daily time
for reading together,
and stick to it.

How bubble gum winds up
in boys' hair no one has ever
figured out.

Don't buy white carpeting. You're just inviting misery.

Enjoy his bath time.
He certainly will.

Tell him your kisses
magically heal skinned
knees. Distribute magic
kisses liberally.

Teach him how to make
a peanut butter sandwich.
This could be his main source
of sustenance for the next
ten years of his life.

Don't forget:
Praise is contagious.
So is criticism.

Play catch with him. He won't really care if you can't catch a ball or throw a perfect pass.

Remember, your encouragement breeds confidence. It always will.

To a young boy,
happiness is a big spoon
and a bowl of chocolate
chip cookie dough.

Teach him to talk with his mouth open and chew with it closed.

He will continually be
fascinated by things he
finds in his body.

He will try to drag a hose from his sandbox into the living room. Discourage this.

Teach him to
check his zipper.

He will want a bike.
He will fall off it.
He will live.

Your purse will always be
a source of mystery
to him.

Take walks with him at his pace.
He could spend five minutes
watching a doodlebug.

Show him how to fold his clothes. But don't expect miracles.

Teach him manners.

Let him teach you
how to skip stones.

Show interest when he brings home yucky stuff. The more scared you act by the worm, frog, or cricket, the happier he'll be.

Don't let his father
forget that his son is
still a little boy.

Don't tolerate
his tantrums.
Ever.

He will always want to show off
his injuries. Act horrified.

Try not to spend time arguing. Make a decision and move on.

No matter how much he protests, put him in his car seat. In the backseat.

Be prepared when taking him shoe shopping. Boys test new shoes by racing down the aisles of the shoe store.

At a certain point in time,
he will think peeing is the
most fun you can possibly
have in life. He'll move on.

Teach him to help you out around the house.

If he comes home filthy and muddy, have no qualms about hosing him off before letting him back inside.

Take him to the store with you.
Let him pick out the juice,
the apples, the cereal.

He will delight in grossing you out.

Let him be a boy.
Don't expect
a "little gentleman"
at age five.

Teach him how to set the table. This will amaze future girlfriends.

Learn to make a good explosion noise. He'll think you're amazingly cool.

You'll think you don't have time to take pictures and keep albums, but you must. They will mean much more to you than videos ever will.

When all else fails,
give him cookies
and milk.

# Sports

Put your fears aside. Even if he's small and slow, he needs to play.

# Always be his cheerleader.

For many years, it won't matter to him if he wins, only that he's playing.

Give him swimming
lessons early. Waterproof
him as a baby.

Generally speaking, your advice in picking out soccer or baseball shoes is not welcome.

Be prepared: The price of his athletic equipment will make you consider taking out a second mortgage.

He'll always look
for you at his games.
Sit where he can see you.

It's okay if you don't love attending his meets. But it's important that you're there cheering when something exciting happens.

Remember,
even perfectly sane moms
tend to freak out
during soccer tryouts.

If he gets cut from a team,
it will be one of the worst days
of his life. And yours.

You will realize early on that there are two kinds of moms: those who coach, and those who never trust their sons' coaches.

If he's old enough to play, he's old enough to carry his own equipment.

He won't understand
if you cry just because
he's bleeding.

Tell him he had a great game, even if there's overwhelming evidence to the contrary. He just needs to hear you say it.

Keep sports fun for
as long as possible.
Remind his dad of this.

# Grade School

Walk him to school for as long as he'll let you.

Give him piano lessons—he'll thank you for them when he's older. But if you're constantly yelling at him to practice, something is wrong. With you.

Remind him that passing gas is hysterically funny only to other boys.

# Expect roughhousing. It's loud, but it's normal.

Remember, boys show their affection by wrestling, pushing, and bumping into one another.

# Don't go nuts
if he messes up.
He's still just a little boy.

Teach him to be kind.

Teach him
the right way to use mouthwash.
Or else he'll swallow it.

Remember,
he's probably hungry.
Even if he just ate.

Teach him to hang up his clothes, even if it's easier to just pick them up yourself.

Don't worry about spending quality time with your son. Just spend *time* with him.

Remember, the greatest gift you can give him is the strength to solve his own problems.

Buy him a chemistry set and help him make something with it. Ooh and aah over how dangerous it is.

Boys love toy cars.
It's inexplicable.

Don't focus on turning him into a man. But don't let him stay a little boy.

When he dresses himself, tell him he looks great. Don't worry about what others might think.

Always, always, always know what he is watching on TV.

Firmly establish the ground rules about his grades. Make sure he knows that they are the number one priority.

Get to know his teachers.
They now spend as much time
with him as you do.

Don't miss his school plays. Even if his role is "Tree #2."

Eat lunch with him.
Find out what's going on
in his world.

Don't try to make
him into the man
you always wanted.

His spontaneous hugs might
stop when he's around eight years
old, but don't worry—
they'll be back.

As wild as they might be, little boys need hugs and security. So do big ones.

When you're at the store
together, teach him about money.
Explain how some things
are too expensive.

Talk to him about saving for the future. Give him a piggy bank.

Picking up after him all the time doesn't show how much you love him. It shows how much he can manipulate you.

Teach him to wipe
his mouth on a napkin,
not on his shirt.

He will want a puppy.
He will love it.
You will clean up after it.

Resolve to spend an hour every day just having fun with him.

He will idolize his dad.

Gently remind him that anything he finds in his nose should, for the good of society, stay there.

He will want you
to feel his muscles.
Tell him he's a hunk.

Join the PTA.
Become a homeroom sponsor.
Volunteer as a classroom aide.
Know what's going on at his school.

Remind him that every single action—good or bad—has a consequence.

Check his backpack nightly. He will let important information die in there.

There will be times when the last thing in the world you want to tell him is "no." But you'll have to.

Teach him to read the instructions. His dad might have missed this.

Have tea with him
in the afternoons.
Serve cookies.

Remember, well-adjusted boys have loving mothers who are a source of strength, not criticism.

Watch your behavior around him: your language, your mores, your alcohol intake. He's watching you, and learning.

Show him how to
hold a baby.

Avoid telling him to walk or talk "normal." Let him be himself.

Instead of trying to control his behavior, learn to gently shape it.

Let him grow up.

The longer
you baby him,
the longer
he'll stay a baby.

D on't get in the habit
of making excuses for him,
or you'll be doing it
for the rest of his life.

Give him a Valentine's Day card every year. He'll say it's corny, but secretly he'll always look forward to it.

He will always
look to you for love.

Teach him how to use
the microwave—without
blowing up the kitchen.

# Never call him names.

You will always feel his pain.
But don't mistake it for your own.

Don't get in the habit of
offering him anything in
the world to make him happy,
or nothing in the world will.

If he's being picked on in school, it's important he solve the problem himself. Advise, but don't interfere. It will just humiliate him and make matters worse.

If there's no one around to teach him how to defend himself, send him to karate lessons.

If you discover that *he's* the bully, realize something is very wrong. Usually at home.

Talk to him about sex and drugs
and alcohol and parties,
even if you think he's too young.
Middle school awaits.

Surprise him by taking him out of school and bringing him to a baseball game.

Occasionally,
let him stay up late
and look at the stars.
He'll never forget it.

# Spirituality

Talk to him often about
God's grace and
he'll grow up seeing it.

Little boys love to bang their feet against the pews during worship. Remove his shoes and he'll sit a lot more quietly.

Teach him his prayers.
Say them with him every
night as a family.

Buy him
a children's bible
and read it with him.

Treat his father with love and respect. Show your son that being a man is a good thing.

One way to get him to go to services peacefully is to let him bring his friends along.

Don't tolerate meanness.

Be consistent
with worship.
Go regularly.

Have him join
a youth group.
He'll like it more
than he'll expect to.

Teach him to start an active prayer life *before* he's sitting in an exam he hasn't studied for.

Don't let him beg off attending worship or religious school. His time there will pay huge dividends down the line.

Say a blessing at every meal. Remind him that even the food he eats is a gift.

Stand up for your morals. Don't give in. He might protest now, but eventually he will model himself after you.

Don't forget that although an active spiritual life doesn't solve all of life's ills, it does prevent quite a few.

Even when he's older,
remind him
to say his prayers.

Make sure his home is a haven of love and peace.

Don't forget that God has given you an awesome responsibility: raising a son in today's world.

# Middle
# School

Remember,
all boys rebel.

Tell yourself,
"He's not angry, he's not
an alien, he's not mental.
He's just 13."

Demand respect.
At all times.

Keep in mind that he's not a child anymore, but he's not an adult, either. Treating him like either one will lead to disaster.

D on't forget:
A teenage boy's brain
is an unfathomable thing.

Keep kissing him
good night.
Even if he doesn't
kiss back.

The single best way to avoid turbulent teenage years is to surround him with love, stability, and family in his formative years.

Don't shield him from the consequences of his bad behavior. Dealing with the aftermath of his actions will make him a better person.

If he's caught
cheating at school,
don't yell at the teacher.
Drop the boom on him.

Ask him who the vice president of the United States is. Make sure he knows about the world he lives in.

Look him in the eye and tell him that if he ever starts doing drugs, his life as he knows it will come to an end.

$I$f he's getting in trouble
at school all the time,
it probably *is* his fault.

Prepare to spend the
next few years in the car,
driving him and
his friends around.

Play Beethoven
in the mornings.
It will calm
everybody down.

State, in your harshest mother-voice, that under no circumstances, in this lifetime, may he jump off any roof into a pool.

Know that left unattended
for one second, however,
he *will* jump off the nearest roof
into the nearest pool.

Establish firm consequences for breaking the rules, and stick to them. You don't have to get mad at him to take away his video games.

Don't be upset that you can't afford everything he wants. A small country couldn't even afford everything he wants.

Know that the longer he spends styling his hair, the goofier it will look.

D on't negotiate
the punishments
for his wrongdoings
*after* he's been caught.

Tell him that studying hard and respecting a teacher's authority are crucial to avoiding problems in school.

Teach him that trust is something that can be lost in the blink of a lie.

Remember,
success breeds success.

He will want you to be his friend. But what he really needs is a mom.

Everything will smell better when he starts using soap. And deodorant. Regularly.

Be assured that fathers have been left alone with their sons for eons, and the human race has continued.

Talk to him. Ask questions. All the time. Let him know you're aware of his life.

If you don't teach him to do his laundry, you'll be doing it for him for as long he lives with you. And probably after.

Remind him not to mix whites with colors unless he wants to wear pink socks to gym class.

$S$pend as much time
as you can with him.

Do not let one
single disrespectful
comment slide.
Ever.

He's ready to learn about girls. He can either learn from you, or from MTV.

Remind him that when he doesn't want to talk to you about something, that's when he most needs to do it.

He'll never stay mad at
you. You're his mom.

Eat dinner as a family as much as possible. Talk about politics, the economy, sports, art—anything engaging. You will grow together.

Make sure he and his dad have time alone together.

He will start using copious
amounts of cologne.
You might have to stagger
outside for air.

Tell him how he can earn your respect: always speaking the truth, keeping his grades up, treating all family members with kindness, doing his chores, and seeking to serve others.

Be a part of his world.
Know what games he plays,
what shows he watches,
what music he's listening to.

Ask yourself: Do you care enough about his growth to *not* let him play violent video games? Don't give in just so you don't have to listen to his whining.

Boys this age will generally try out rude behavior on their moms that they wouldn't dare try on their dads. Don't allow it.

Tell his dad that it's time for him to talk with his son about sex. Understand that neither will be crazy about the idea.

Don't let him make fun
of other people.

Make sure he does volunteer work. It's a proven way for him to stop thinking about only himself.

Never let him get the idea that he's the boss.

# Teach him
# how to sew on a button.

Don't miss attending
a performance or an event
or a game that he's involved in.

Make sure he knows that girls can do anything boys can do.

Remember, your job isn't to do everything for him. It's to teach him how to do things for himself.

Teach him
never to be satisfied
with the status quo.

If his grades slip, make him study in front of you, at the kitchen table. His grades will improve dramatically.

Remember, it's *his* homework. Check to make sure he's done it, but don't do it for him.

Don't judge his fun by what appeals to you. Most boys are more aggressive, thrill-seeking, and daring than their moms are.

If you don't believe in him, it will be hard for him to believe in himself.

Feed his friends. You'll learn about them—and your son—as they raid the fridge.

# Be unified
# with his father.

Keep in mind that he's listening to every word you say. Especially when you say something negative.

Don't ask his teachers for special favors. They'll think of your son as someone whose mom is looking after him. That kind of reputation will follow him for years.

He will be capable of eating a huge dinner, going out with his buddies, and—an hour later— eating dinner again. It's normal.

Be strong.
This is not the time in
his life to relax the rules.

If he complains that other kids get a bigger allowance or more things, don't give in. He'll live.

Show him how
to boil water.
He thinks he knows how.
He doesn't.

Buy him food he can make himself: sandwich stuff, oatmeal, canned soup.

Make sure he eats his spinach. And anything else you cook for him.

Don't let him hurry through dinner and leave once he's finished. Have him sit at the table until everyone else is done, too. Then have him help clean up.

Accept the fact that he'll be in a bad mood for the next three years.

When planning a family vacation, think ski slopes and beaches instead of museums and sightseeing. Boys are restless.

Don't forget, he needs to know you're always there. No matter how weird he gets.

Remember, he's always testing the boundaries. Think long and hard before letting them move so much as an inch.

Every now and then
go into his room,
sit down, and just visit.

Insist that he
let you know where he is
at all times.

Encourage him to read:
sports pages,
skateboarding magazines,
Shakespeare—
as long as he's reading.

Remember, in middle school you can bar unsafe peers from his life. In high school, you can only bar them from your house.

# Girls

If he becomes paralyzed when a girl says hello, you'll know he's discovered the opposite sex.

Don't push him into
a romantic relationship. Not now.
Not ten years from now.
Not ever.

If he starts calling girls derogatory names, it's time for a stern heart-to-heart.

# Inevitably,
a girl will break his heart.

He might start middle school a good foot shorter than most girls. Don't worry. He'll grow.

Remember, boys show affection
to girls by teasing them,
wrestling with them, and generally
annoying them. Girls somehow
get the message anyway.

Keep in mind that in adolescence, being able to say that he has a girlfriend is more important than the actual girlfriend.

Don't let him spend
every dime he's earned
on her.

He will need you to explain the way girls think. His dad can't help him here.

Don't even think of sending him to a party without knowing who will be there, and making sure that the host's parents will be home.

You can't stop him from falling for a girl whose life is in chaos. But you can explain what her life is doing to his.

Television is teaching him that women are promiscuous and shallow, and only want to date athletes or rock stars. He needs you to correct this impression.

Be careful not to attach special meaning to any of his girlfriends. They will come and go.

Remind him to buy
his prom date a corsage.
Remind him several times.

Don't be surprised when the girl
he introduces as his future wife
is uncannily similar to you.

# High School

Believe in him.
More than he believes
in himself.

Remember, you're still one of his most important role models.

Praise him for his qualities, not only his accomplishments.

Try to see things
from his point of view.
Sometimes.

Make sure he knows that his grades matter more than ever now.

Tell him often what it is
you respect about him.

Find out what motivates him, what inspires him, what fires him up.

Don't expect all his actions to make sense. In many ways, he's still a child.

If he knows he can come to you with a problem, he will.

Appreciate his accomplishments. Your opinion means everything to him.

Learn the difference between supporting him and rescuing him.

# Hold him accountable
# for his actions.

He will always need you when he is in pain—emotionally, spiritually, or physically. Always.

If he loses your trust,
let him earn it again.

Expect success.
Expectations have a way
of becoming reality.

Don't be the "cool mom" who permits underage drinking. You're giving him the message that it's okay to break the law. And that you don't care about what he does.

Don't be quick to give him cash every time he asks for it. You're teaching him to rely on you for money, instead of earning it himself.

Don't feel sorry for him.
That doesn't do him any
long-term favors.

Remember,
he will resist maturity
for as long as you let him.

If you have a fixation
on brands and labels,
he will too.

Don't be concerned with him disliking you. Instead, be concerned with him respecting you.

To your amazement, he will want clothes that cost more than his dad's do. This is when you sit him down and explain the concept of getting a job.

Don't let him tell you that he doesn't have time for a job. He has time.

Remind yourself that you can't buy his love.

Enforce
the consequences
of bad behavior.

If you're criticizing
him constantly,
the problem is you.

Remember, low grades are one of the first indicators that something is wrong.

Make him talk to you.
Don't let him
shut you out of his life.

He will want to talk
at the most odd, mysterious,
inconvenient times.
Stop what you're doing and talk.

Realize that his friends are vitally important to him right now. Condemning them will only alienate him from you.

When he first gets his driver's license, he *will* get lost. Make sure he has a cell phone.

When he's driving and you're in the passenger seat, don't scream, have a panic attack, or claim he's trying to kill you. Be calm. Be calm.

He doesn't need
a radar detector.
If he's getting speeding tickets,
he needs to slow down.

If he does get a ticket,
don't try to get it fixed.
Send him to court.
Wearing a tie.

Keep him busy
outside of school—reading,
sports, clubs, lessons, a job—
it means he has less time to find
ways to get in trouble.

Take him to the theater.
Have him drive.

# Remind him to smile.

Talk to his
friends' parents.
Find out what's going
on over there.

Remember, if he smells odd to you, he smells odd to the world.

There will come a time when he'll urge you to dress like the girls his age. Ignore him.

Don't hold him back.
Let him be independent.

Make sure he knows that who he can be doesn't depend on who he has been.

If it's dangerous,
life-threatening,
and makes no sense,
he will love it. Brace yourself.

Don't defend
his mistakes.

Insist he pick up after himself. Don't tolerate him being a slob.

Tell him
you're proud of him.
Tell him why.

Never treat him as your parent, husband, or best friend. He's your son.

Never allow his
emotions to rule
the house.

Talk about the future.
Find out what he sees
himself doing with his life.

Even throughout college,
he will think money grows
on trees. Correct his thinking.

Never buy the argument
that none of his friends
have curfews.

Learn to listen
without judgment.
Or even talking.

Don't take everything he says to heart. Boys like to try out ideas on their moms, then merrily go out and play while their mothers lie in shock on their beds.

Teach him to write thank you notes. It will serve him for the rest of his life.

He will spend hours obsessing over cars you will never buy for him. It's a guy thing.

Remind him that each time he loses his integrity, it becomes harder and harder to find.

Apologize to him when you screw up.

Teach him that sharing
what he has is one of the
keys to happiness.

Don't simply criticize
what's on TV.
Unplug the set.

Realize he may choose a college because it:

a) is known as a great party school
b) attracts the best-looking women
c) has a beach nearby

Help him get his priorities straight.

Your heart will break whenever he's unhappy. This will be true pretty much forever.

His weekend nights might start later, but the curfew still applies.

Insist he watch his language around you.

Fix him snacks
when he's up late studying.
It will help keep him going.

Remember,
the stronger a mother you are,
the stronger a man
he will become.

Treat him like the man
you want him to become.

Refuse to feed him until he completes his college applications. That will motivate him.

# Leaving Home

Ask him to please never get a tattoo involving the word *Mom*.

$T$ell him you will
always love him.

Remind him
that beer is not one
of the major food groups.

He will tell you
that you're the
best mom in the world.

Hug him fiercely.

Tell him to call you.

Remember, he'll be back.
He's hungry.

Let him go.